Scotland

by Jessica Rudolph

Consultant: Marjorie Faulstich Orellana, PhD
Professor of Urban Schooling
University of California, Los Angeles

WITHDRAWN

BEARPORT PUBLISHING

New York, New York

Credits

Cover, © shapecharge/iStock and © lowsun/Shutterstock; TOC, © Rosa Jay/Shutterstock; 4, © matthewleesdixon/iStock; 5T, © Paolo Gallo/Shutterstock; 5B, © chris148/iStock; 7, © Milosz Maslanka/Shutterstock; 8–9, © Loop Images Ltd/Alamy Stock Photo; 9R, © Paul White Aerial views/Alamy Stock Photo; 10L, © Matt84/iStock; 10–11, © Bucchi Francesco/Shutterstock; 11R, © MichaelTaylor3d/Shutterstock; 12, © elvisvaughn/Shutterstock; 13, © Derek Croucher/Alamy Stock Photo; 14, © Look and Learn/Bridgeman Images; 15, © PA Images/Alamy Stock Photo; 16, © Shaiith/iStock; 17T, © jan kranendonk/Shutterstock; 17B, © Iain Sharp/Alamy Stock Photo; 18, © Shaiith/iStock; 19T, © antonioscarpi/iStock; 19B, © Richard Wood/Alamy Stock Photo; 20, © Simon Greig/Shutterstock; 21, © bikeriderlondon/Shutterstock; 22, © Stockbyte/Thinkstock; 22–23, © Peter Burnett/iStock; 24T, Public Domain; 24B, © C. and M. History Pictures/Alamy Stock Photo; 25T, Public Domain; 25BL, © SilverScreen/Alamy Stock Photo; 25BR, © Look and Learn/Bridgeman Images; 26, © Stocksolutions/Dreamstime; 27, © edenexposed/iStock; 28, © JASPERIMAGE/Shutterstock; 29, © myrrha/iStock; 30T, © Robert Chlopas/Dreamstime; 30B, © Iain Sarjeant/Alamy Stock Photo; 31 (T to B), © Microgen/Shutterstock, © f11photo/Shutterstock, © Matt84/iStock, © Paolo Gallo/Shutterstock, © HandmadePictures/Shutterstock, and © Travel Stock/Shutterstock; 32, © chrisdorney/Shutterstock.

Publisher: Kenn Goin
Editor: J. Clark
Creative Director: Spencer Brinker
Design: Debrah Kaiser
Photo Researcher: Thomas Persano

Library of Congress Cataloging-in-Publication Data

Names: Rudolph, Jessica, author.
Title: Scotland / by Jessica Rudolph.
Description: New York, New York : Bearport Publishing, [2018] | Series:
   Countries we come from | Includes bibliographical references and index. |
   Audience: Ages 5–8.
Identifiers: LCCN 2017000875 (print) | LCCN 2017001371 (ebook) | ISBN
   9781684022557 (library) | ISBN 9781684023097 (ebook)
Subjects: LCSH: Scotland—Juvenile literature.
Classification: LCC DA762 .R83 2018 (print) | LCC DA762 (ebook) | DDC
   941.1—dc23
LC record available at https://lccn.loc.gov/2017000875

Copyright © 2018 Bearport Publishing Company, Inc. All rights reserved. No part of this publication may be reproduced in whole or in part, stored in any retrieval system, or transmitted in any form or by any means, electronic, mechanical, photocopying, recording, or otherwise, without written permission from the publisher.

For more information, write to Bearport Publishing Company, Inc., 45 West 21st Street, Suite 3B, New York, New York 10010. Printed in the United States of America.

10 9 8 7 6 5 4 3 2 1

Contents

This Is Scotland

RUGGED

Traditional

Busy

Scotland is a country in Europe.

It's located on a large island called Great Britain.

Scotland shares the island with England and Wales.

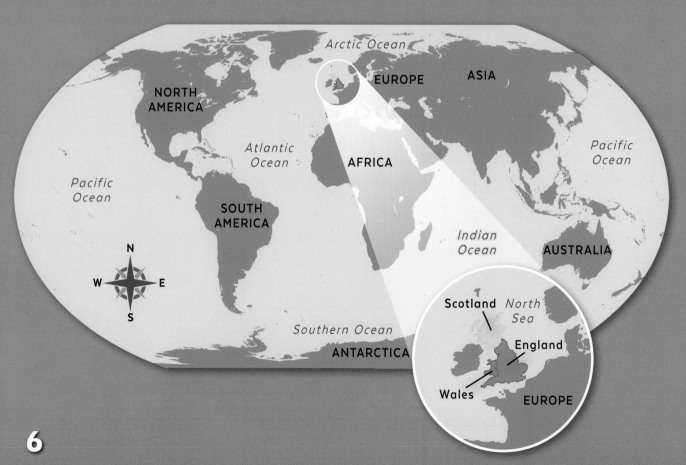

Arctic Ocean

EUROPE

ASIA

NORTH AMERICA

Atlantic Ocean

AFRICA

Pacific Ocean

Pacific Ocean

SOUTH AMERICA

Indian Ocean

AUSTRALIA

N

W   E

S

Southern Ocean

ANTARCTICA

Scotland   *North Sea*

England

Wales

EUROPE

More than five million people live in Scotland. Scottish people are often called Scots.

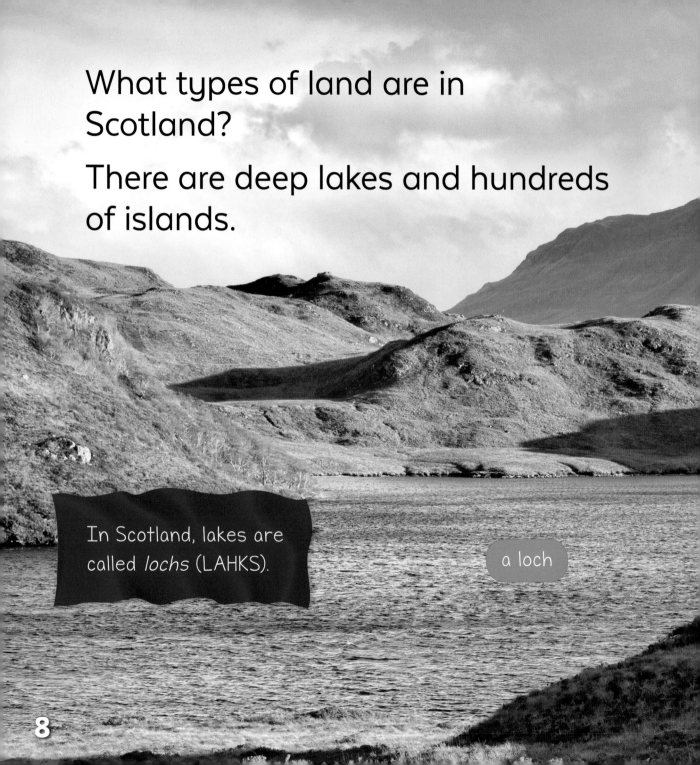

What types of land are in Scotland?

There are deep lakes and hundreds of islands.

In Scotland, lakes are called *lochs* (LAHKS).

a loch

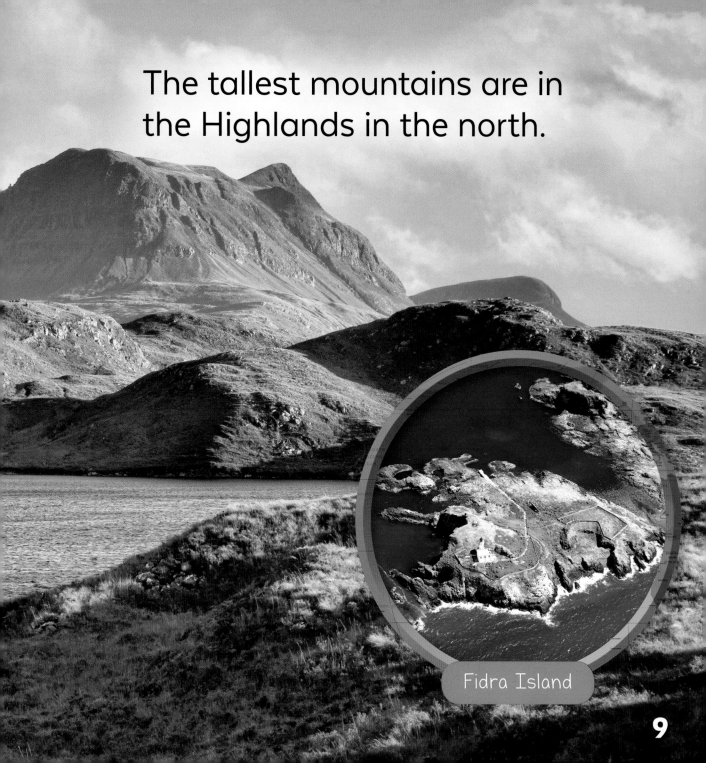

The tallest mountains are in the Highlands in the north.

Fidra Island

Scotland's most famous lake is Loch Ness.

It's said to be the home of the Loch Ness Monster, or Nessie.

There have been many reported sightings of Nessie.

Yet no one has proven that the giant creature exists.

This photo was taken in 1934. Could it be Nessie?

a plesiosaur

Some people say the
monster is related to
a dinosaur. Others
think it's a **hoax**.

visitors to
Loch Ness

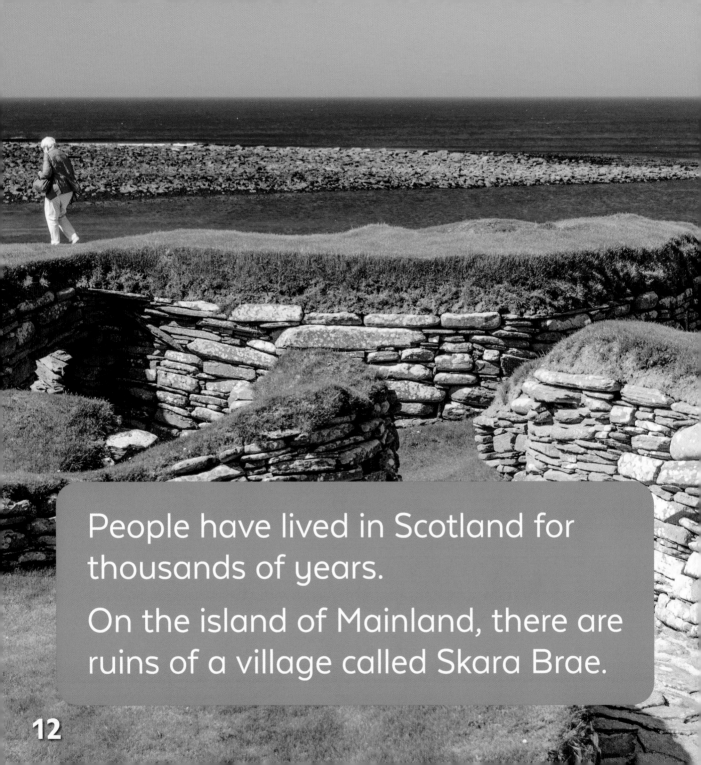

People have lived in Scotland for thousands of years.

On the island of Mainland, there are ruins of a village called Skara Brae.

In the stone houses, **archaeologists** found tables, beds, and even toilets!

The ruins of Skara Brae are 5,000 years old.

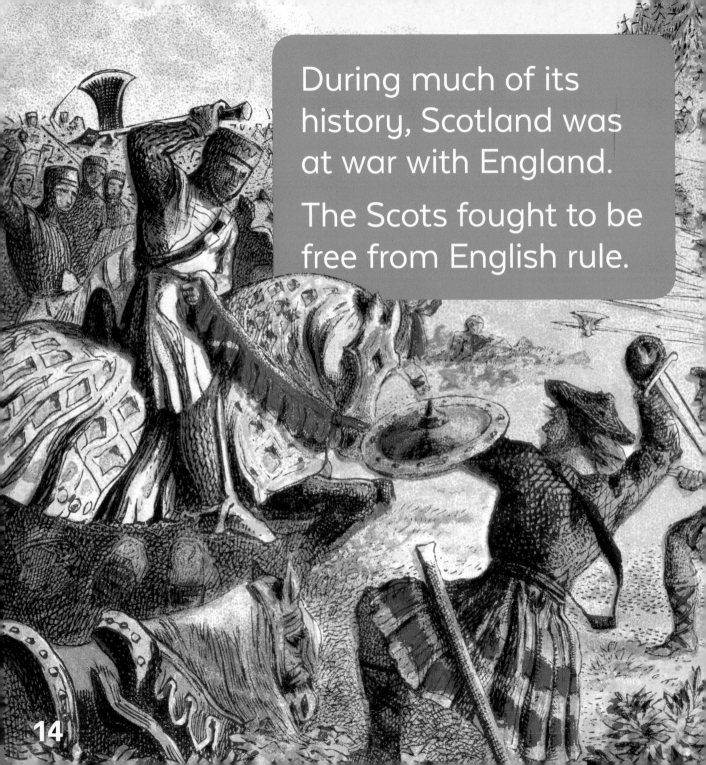

During much of its history, Scotland was at war with England.

The Scots fought to be free from English rule.

14

In 1707, England and Scotland agreed to form one government.

Finally, there was peace.

Today, Scotland and England are part of a nation called the United Kingdom. However, Scotland also has its own government.

Scotland's **capital** is Edinburgh (ED-in-*bur*-uh).

There's a lot to do there.

People can tour Edinburgh Castle.

Edinburgh Castle was built in the 1100s.

They can also go to festivals that celebrate music and art.

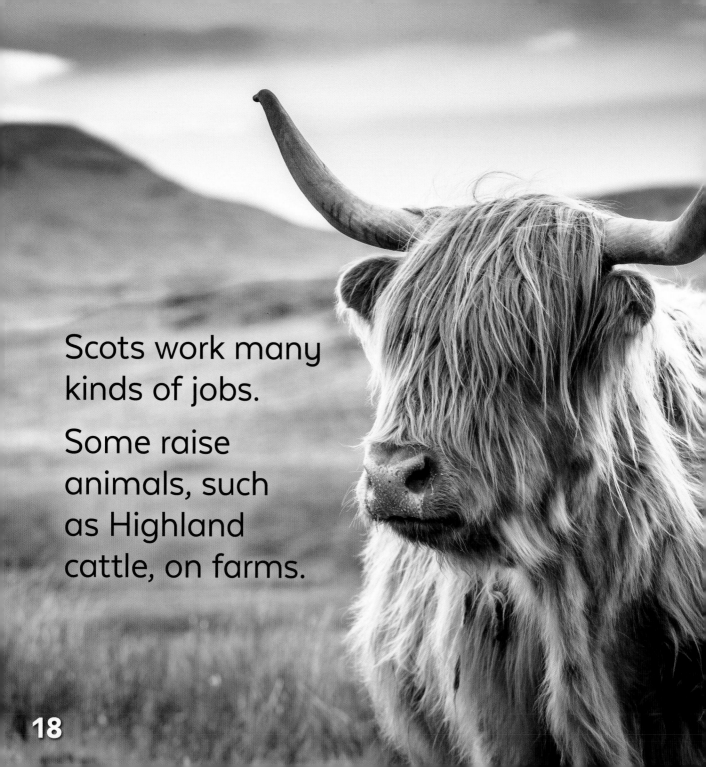

Scots work many kinds of jobs.

Some raise animals, such as Highland cattle, on farms.

Others fish for haddock
and mackerel in the ocean.

Many Scottish people work
on **oil rigs**. They drill for oil at
the bottom of the North Sea.

Most people in Scotland speak English.

Some people also speak Scottish Gaelic.

In Gaelic, this is how you say *My name is*:

'S mise
(SMIH-shuh)

a sign written in English and Scottish Gaelic

Welcome to Scotland
Fàilte gu Alba

Many people also speak Scots. Scots words include *lassie* and *laddie*. These words mean "girl" and "boy."

Scotland is well known for the bagpipes.

This instrument is played at parades and other events.

It has an eerie, droning sound and can be heard miles away.

kilt

Bagpipers usually wear traditional Scottish **kilts**.

Many famous writers have come from Scotland.

In 1904, J. M. Barrie wrote a play called *Peter Pan*.

Barrie

It's about a boy who can fly and never grows up.

Doyle

In the late 1800s, Arthur Conan Doyle created stories about a detective named Sherlock Holmes. Many movies and TV shows have been made about him.

The national food of Scotland is haggis.

This dish is made of **minced** sheep's organs, oatmeal, and seasonings.

The ingredients are boiled in the stomach of a sheep.

For dessert, many Scots eat delicious Dundee cakes. They're made with fruits and almonds.

The Highland Games are athletic competitions held across Scotland every year.

The most difficult event is the caber toss.

Athletes toss a long tree trunk that can weigh up to 175 pounds (79 kg)!

Other events include the hammer throw and the tug-of-war.

Fast Facts

Capital city: Edinburgh

Population of Scotland: More than five million

Main languages: English, Scottish Gaelic, Scots

Money: Pound

Major religion: Christianity

Neighboring country: England

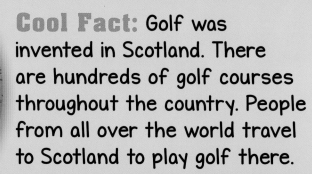

Cool Fact: Golf was invented in Scotland. There are hundreds of golf courses throughout the country. People from all over the world travel to Scotland to play golf there.

archaeologists (ar-kee-AHL-uh-jists) scientists who learn about ancient times by studying things they dig up, such as tools

capital (KAP-uh-tuhl) a city where a country's government is based

hoax (HOHKS) a trick that makes people believe something that is not true

kilts (KILTS) knee-length skirts worn by Scottish men

minced (MINSD) cut up into very small pieces

oil rigs (OYL RIGZ) platforms used to drill for oil beneath the ocean floor

Index

Read More

Yomtov, Nel. *Scotland (Enchantment of the World).* New York: Children's Press (2015).

Zobel, Derek. *Scotland (Blastoff! Readers: Exploring Countries).* Minneapolis, MN: Bellwether Media (2012).

Learn More Online

To learn more about Scotland, visit
www.bearportpublishing.com/CountriesWeComeFrom

About the Author

Jessica Rudolph lives in Connecticut. She has edited and written many books about history, science, and nature for children.